A RIVER RUNNING THROUGH YOU

amy-jane beer

elin manon

and the rivers running through them

MAGIC CAT PUBLISHING

Have you ever lingered on a riverbank watching the water flow, and wondered where it comes from, or where it might be going?

These are *very* old questions.

And old questions often have stories for answers.

If you could follow the water everywhere it goes, you would find yourself on a never-ending journey through time and space.

A river is water's chance to dance under the Sun,
and to speak its stories.

What might it tell you about the places it has been?

The water in your river has crossed many oceans.

Rivers in the ocean are called currents and gyres.
They are highways for creatures making epic journeys of their own.

Seawater is salty because it has spent billions of years collecting minerals washed from the land by all the rivers of the world.

The flow could tell you a tale
of rivers in the sky.

Energy from the Sun warms surface water until some molecules are released into the air. They can travel huge distances, invisibly.

When water vapour cools, it shrinks into droplets of liquid or crystals of ice, forming clouds or fog.

If those droplets and crystals grow big enough, they become raindrops, snowflakes or hail,

and

down

they

come

again,

to Earth.

What does the water remember of ages past,
when it held the land in an icy embrace?

When it is very cold for a really long time, water is compressed into glaciers, rivers of ice that flow . . .

so slowly . . .

that the movement is only noticeable over years.

The flow in your river has dwelt for long ages
underground, where in darkness
it crept and pooled . . .

and
cascaded
deep
inside the
Earth . . .

to be reborn, again and again.

What might water whisper
of tiny rivers that seep in
soil and moss and trees?

How long did the water wait
in pools and lakes . . .

The largest lakes delay water on its journey for a hundred years or more.

in bogs . . .

Bogs form in areas where water is held by beautiful peat mosses.

in swamps, marshes and fens . . .

Where water gathers in low-lying places, it feeds reedbeds, meres and mudflats teeming with life.

Listen. The river might share a secret.
You are the many times great-grandchild
of a fish it once knew.

The water that held the fish
is also running through you.

But water is only with us for a short time before it moves on to become something else.

Our long-ago ancestors lived in water for billions of years before some unusual fish began using their fins as limbs to crawl, instead of swim.

Each of us begins our lives in a safe, dark pool of womb-water called amniotic fluid. Like the sea where all life began, it is warm and salty.

Your river has lived uncounted lives
and each one is an adventure.

Water-loving willows are a gift of nature,
providing food, medicine and shelter
to a host of other beings.

Young salmon go to sea to grow, but never forget their home river.
They battle the flow to return and begin a new cycle of life.

Kingfishers hunt from perches
overhanging the flow, diving faster
than the eye can see.

Mayflies spend most of their lives underwater,
emerging to dance on newly unfurled wings
for a single, magical day.

Stories about rivers help us understand what it means to be alive and ever-changing.

The spirits of river-stories are often both beautiful and frightening. They show that our ancestors understand water to be essential and dangerous.

Some stories describe mixed up creatures – half fish, half-human. Others tell of shapeshifters able to change their form as water does.

Most water on our planet is salty, frozen or hidden deep underground. Only a precious fraction flows fresh and free in rivers, lakes and living beings, like you.

Rivers are often the reason we live, farm and build in particular places. We use them for energy, transport, to grow food and to wash away our waste.

Sometimes the things people do harm rivers, and many times we have fought over them, harming each other.

Rivers often mark borders and boundaries between people and countries.

But sometimes we fight *for* them.

Knowing and loving your river and the lives it carries
gives you the power to protect them.

One day your river will return from its wandering to a place like the one where you stand, wondering.

But it won’t be the same river, because
everything changes, including you.

Water is patient.

In time, it can move mountains.
Grain by grain.
Pebble by pebble.

Even rock eventually wears away to become something else.
But rivers remain . . .
passing through . . .
moving on . . .

connecting lives, and places,
and making the impossible . . .

possible.

MAGIC CAT PUBLISHING

A River Running Through You

First Published in 2026 by Magic Cat Publishing, an imprint of Lucky Cat Publishing Ltd,
Unit 2 Empress Works, 24 Grove Passage, London E2 9FQ, UK
EU Authorised Representative Magic Cat Publishing, an imprint of Lucky Cat Publishing Ltd,
PAKTA svetovanje d.o.o., Stegne 33, Ljubljana, Slovenia

A catalogue record for this book is available from the British Library.

ISBN 978-1-917366-30-4

The illustrations were created digitally
Set in Im Fell Double Pica and the secret things

Published by Rachel Williams and Jenny Broom
Designed by Kim Hankinson
Edited by Jenny Broom

Manufactured in China

9 8 7 6 5 4 3 2 1

MIX
Paper | Supporting responsible forestry
FSC® C104723
FSC www.fsc.org

'For Lochy, who is part otter, and our river, the Yorkshire Derwent.'

amy-jane beer

'To all our storytellers and campaigners, for your tireless work in the celebration, protection and restoration of our precious rivers – thank you.'

elin manon